POPE FRANCIS

Migrants and Refugees

WITNESSES TO HOPE

United State~
Conference of Cath~

Originally published in Italian, as "*Sono Io, Non Abbiate Paura,*"
Parole Di Papa Francesco Su Rifugiati E Migranti (LEV, 2018).

Cover image: CNS/Paul Haring.

First printing, October 2018

ISBN 978-1-60137-609-1

Introduction

Fr. Michael Czerny, SJ[1]

In the middle of the night, during a storm at sea, the boat was many furlongs distant from the land, beaten by the waves. Jesus seemed to be elsewhere and, the wind against them, the disciples were rowing desperately. "They were frightened" and for good reason.[2] Some were experienced fishermen, yet they were all afraid because the dark and dangerous waters and the contrary weather made them very anxious, vulnerable and insecure.

Like the disciples on a stormy night at sea, migrants and refugees often feel like they are travelling "in the dark." They face many difficulties, without being sure of when or where they'll arrive and what awaits them there. They are afraid, and the reasons for their fears are easy for anyone to understand. Even after their arrival, no longer in need of protection from the immediate threat of harm, many refugees and migrants "are afraid of confrontation, judgment, discrimination, failure." Pope Francis acknowledges, "These fears are legitimate."[3]

In the middle of another night, Jesus tells us, a friend is knocking on the door asking to borrow food for an unexpected guest. From inside the house, the head of the family shouts back, "Do not bother me; the door is now shut, and my children are with me in bed."[4] We readily imagine this situation of normal daily life, a secure and tranquil domestic scene, now being rudely disturbed. Our sympathies can lie on both sides of the door, so to speak: with the friend in need, and with the family who is usually hospitable but resents the disruption.

We may have a similar mix of feelings when asylum seekers and migrants are "knocking on the door in the middle of the night"—in our communities and in our countries. Why might some residents and some communities hesitate to "get out of bed and open the door"? There are different worries that prevent us from "opening the door." Some are worried that criminals or terrorists might inevitably get in. For others, it's that newcomers, needing to work, might take away our jobs; or if they don't work, they drain our social services. Others ask themselves, "What if these people fall victim to criminal organizations that exploit them, what is the point in them coming to live as slaves?" Or they might argue that migration is a business built on the lives of the poor, which must be stopped. Some say, "There are too many of them already; we simply cannot afford to accept more." Foreign influences could fundamentally change our way of life, or undermine our culture, or threaten our economic stability. As Pope Francis says: "Local communities are sometimes afraid that the newly arrived will disturb the established order, will 'steal' something they have long labored to build up."[5] Unfortunately, initial negative reactions such as these often persist in spite of an absence of evidence or in the face of evidence to the contrary.

No one is immune from attitudes or reactions such as these. Pope Francis sympathizes: "These are fears which we understand and cannot dismiss lightly."[6] He does not underestimate the difficulties or gloss them over. The Pope told community leaders and local authorities that "I understand the unease of many of our citizens in the face of the arrival of migrants and refugees."[7] Pope Francis shows compassion for people's real fears—and he includes the fears both of local communities and of migrants; the fears of one group should not be played off against the fears of another more vulnerable group.

Still, the "reasons" for hesitating are not always reasonable. This is the context of mixed feelings in which the newly elected Pope Francis made his first trip outside Rome. In July 2013, from the deck of an Italian coastguard vessel, Pope Francis cast a wreath of flowers into the sea off Lampedusa in memory of those who died attempting to cross from North Africa. For the recently elected Holy Father, it was a moment of mourning as well as an opportunity "to challenge people's consciences and lead them to reflection and a concrete change of heart. . . . Let us ask the Lord for the grace to weep over our indifference, to weep over the cruelty of our world, of our own hearts."[8] What should we reflect upon and weep for?

- Every human being shares the same fundamental dignity as a child of God, made in his image and likeness. On reflection we might discover that fear is blocking our moral duty to protect another's inalienable dignity.

- "Mistrust and fear of the other, the foreigner, those who are different" lead to "manifestations of intolerance, discrimination and xenophobia." Such "defensive and negative reactions [are] supposedly justified by a vague moral obligation to preserve an established religious and cultural identity."[9]

- Fear deadens our ability to recognise Jesus in the stranger and respond with the charity of solidarity: "We need the Spirit's prompting, lest we be paralyzed by fear and excessive caution, lest we grow used to keeping within safe bounds."[10]

- "I think that fear is the worst counsellor of countries that tend to close their borders,"[11] of communities that close their gates, of men and women who close their hearts.

- The challenge of welcoming vulnerable migrants "must be addressed in an intelligent and creative way, so that the rights and needs of all are respected and upheld . . . If misunderstanding and fear prevail, something of ourselves dies, our cultures, history and traditions are weakened, and our own peace is compromised."[12]

- "Having doubts and fears is not a sin. The sin is to allow these fears to determine our responses, to limit our choices, to compromise respect and generosity, to feed hostility and rejection. The sin is to refuse to encounter the other, the different, the neighbor, when this is in fact a privileged opportunity to encounter the Lord."[13]

"Fear not" is not a utopian, ingenuous suggestion. The overwhelming experience in countless parishes and communities is of newcomers being welcomed and making a positive contribution both for their own families and for the host population. Of course, there may be unhappy experiences and troubling outcomes as well, and everyone involved (government, Church, civil society, media, the newly arrived themselves) should work hard to prevent them. Misinformation selects, exaggerates and spreads the negative, whereas more accurate information provides a realistic picture open to the future.[14] Resisting this, we understand Pope Francis's invitation to try, take risks, and see what happens. With no certainties but making way for grace to allow the joy of the Gospel to work within us.

The Holy Father's teaching applies both to those who are arriving and to the communities in which they arrive, recognizing everyone's fears and inviting them to remain open and exercise their responsibility. "For new arrivals, to welcome, to know and to acknowledge means to know and respect the laws, the culture and the traditions of the countries that take them in. It even includes understanding their fears and apprehensions for the future. And for local communities to welcome, to know and to acknowledge newcomers means to open themselves without prejudices to their rich diversity, to understand the hopes and potential of the newly arrived as well as their fears and vulnerabilities."[15]

Along with the positive experiences that give us hope, a particular virtue is required: prudence. Prudence is a mark of all sound government, and here it is the virtue to govern and manage a just response to refugee and migrant flows. With prudence, "a country must welcome as many refugees as it can integrate: integrate, that is, educate, provide work . . ."[16] Prudence has to make the calculation, balancing difficulties and needs with capacities and resources. The Pope's teaching in this area rules out inaction and balances compassion with prudence:

> By practising the virtue of prudence, government leaders should take practical measures to welcome, promote, protect, integrate and, "within the limits allowed by a correct understanding of

the common good, to permit [them] to become part of a new society." Leaders have a clear responsibility towards their own communities, whose legitimate rights and harmonious development they must ensure, lest they become like the rash builder who miscalculated and failed to complete the tower he had begun to construct.[17]

Prudence means taking up, both seriously and responsibly, the benefits, the costs and the requirements of genuine integration. Prudence cannot be invoked as an excuse to block those who very much need to come. Prudence can adequately take into account "the needs of the human family and the welfare of each . . ."[18]

Prudence, integration, the common good, and virtuous government are demanding standards. They do not allow for a facile "No, go away." On the contrary, groups and societies which devote the effort and engagement needed to successfully integrate newcomers often discover that they can and wish to welcome even more.

In light of this view (and the book you are now holding), the Pope's teaching goes much farther than "let them in" versus "keep them out." He provides a solid, practical guide to compassion in action. The proper human, Christian response to asylum seekers and vulnerable migrants comprises four active verbs, four things to do and keep on doing: *to welcome, to protect, to promote,* and *to integrate*.[19] "Among the most pressing of the humanitarian issues facing the international community at present is the need to welcome, protect, promote and integrate all those fleeing from war and hunger, or forced by discrimination, persecution, poverty and environmental degradation to leave their homelands."[20]

These four verbs have been expanded into *20 Pastoral Action Points*,[21] which are what the local Church, parishes, Catholic and other organizations, and others can do to help—personally, practically, spiritually, and institutionally. The same *20 Action Points* have also been expressed in governmental language and submitted by the Church as its contribution to the 2018 United Nations Global Compacts on Refugees and for Safe, Orderly and Regular Migration.

Although the terminology of the four verbs is recent, the Church already has a great deal of practical experience with welcoming, protecting, promoting, and integrating vulnerable people on the move. The commitment, as St. Paul VI would have said, is to each person and to the whole person. And Pope Francis has repeatedly invited the local Church to walk the talk: "May every parish, every religious community, every monastery, every shrine of Europe welcome one [refugee] family, beginning with my Diocese of Rome."[22]

With his teachings, in word and deed, Pope Francis prods us to respond with the full compassion of our warm hearts, and with prudence that guides us to do all we can with foresight and skill. His rich framework of *welcome, protect, promote,* and *integrate* may be new; but the inspiration goes back thousands of years into the heart of Christianity.

- Jesus, walking on the sea and drawing near to the boat, called out to the disciples exhausted from rowing against the wind, "Fear not, it is I!"
- When the Good Samaritan stopped to help the injured traveler, he might well have said, "Don't be afraid, you'll be OK, I'll make sure of it." He tended his wounds, brought him to safety and, paying the innkeeper, took charge of his needs.
- When we welcome, feed, and clothe Jesus in the guise of bedraggled, hungry, imperilled migrants and refugees,[23] we pacify their fears and, at the same time, help to dispel the anxieties of our communities not to mention our own personal fears too.
- And if we round out the parable of the unexpected guest at night, we can imagine that, after being disturbed and getting up and giving their neighbor the bread he needed, the family went back to bed content and actually slept better than usual . . . the

next morning, there was still more than enough for breakfast.

As you read the texts in this collection, please pause upon each page and listen in your heart, "Fear not, it is I!"

Notes

1 Undersecretary, Migrants and Refugees Section, Dicastery for Promoting Integral Human Development of the Holy See. The author thanks Fr. Giacomo Costa S.J., Mr. Paolo Foglizzo (Milan) and Mr. Robert Czerny (Ottawa) for help with the writing and editing.

2 Mt 14:22-27, Mk 6:47-52; Jn 6:16-21.

3 Homily January 14, 2018.

4 Lk 11:5-9.

5 Homily January 14, 2018.

6 *Address*, Presentation of Letters of Credence, May 19, 2016.

7 *Address* to the National Association of Italian Municipalities, September 30, 2017.

8 Homily, July 8, 2013.

9 *Address* to CCEE National Directors of Pastoral Care for Migrants, September 22, 2017.

10 *Gaudete et Exsultate*, no. 133.

11 Press conference on flight from Sweden, November 1, 2016.

12 Address, Presentation of Letters of Credence, May 19, 2016.

13 Homily January 14, 2018.

14 The Migrants & Refugees website (*https://migrants-refugees.va/*) offers accurate and realistic information of this sort.

15 Homily January 14, 2018.

16 Press Conference, Geneva-Rome, June 21, 2018.

17 *Message* for the 51st World Day of Peace, January 1, 2018, quoting *Pacem in Terris*, no. 106, and Luke 14:28-30.

18 *Message* for the 51st World Day of Peace, January 1, 2018.

19 The four verbs are drawn from: 2018 Migrant and Refugees Message with the theme, "Welcoming, protecting, promoting and integrating migrants and refugees"; the idea of "welcome" in the homily of January 14, 2018; and part 4, *Four mileposts for action*, in the 2018 Peace Message.

20 *Address*, Presentation of Letters of Credence, May 17, 2018.

21 *https://migrants-refugees.va/20-action-points-migrants*.

22 Angelus September 6, 2015.

23 Mt 25:31-46.

Message for the World Day of Migrants and Refugees (2014)

Migrants and Refugees: Toward a Better World

Dear Brothers and Sisters,

Our societies are experiencing, in an unprecedented way, processes of mutual interdependence and interaction on the global level. While not lacking problematic or negative elements, these processes are aimed at improving the living conditions of the human family, not only economically, but politically and culturally as well. Each individual is a part of humanity and, with the entire family of peoples, shares the hope of a better future. This consideration inspired the theme I have chosen for the World Day of Migrants and Refugees this year: *Migrants and Refugees: Toward a Better World.*

In our changing world, the growing phenomenon of human mobility emerges, to use the words of Pope Benedict XVI, as a "sign of the times" (cf. *Message for the 2006 World Day of Migrants and Refugees*). While it is true that migrations often reveal failures and shortcomings on the part of States and the international community, they also point to the aspiration of humanity to enjoy a unity marked by respect for differences, by attitudes of acceptance and hospitality which enable an equitable sharing of the world's goods, and by the protection and the advancement of the dignity and centrality of each human being.

From the Christian standpoint, the reality of migration, like other human realities, points to the tension between the beauty of creation, marked by Grace and the Redemption, and the mystery of sin. Solidarity, acceptance, and signs of fraternity and understanding exist side by side with rejection, discrimination, trafficking and exploitation, suffering and death. Particularly disturbing are those situations where migration is not only involuntary, but actually set in motion by various forms of human trafficking and enslavement. Nowadays, "slave labor" is common coin! Yet despite the problems, risks and difficulties to be faced, great numbers of migrants and refugees continue to be inspired by confidence and hope; in their hearts they long for a better future, not only for themselves but for their families and those closest to them.

What is involved in the creation of "a better world"? The expression does not allude naively to abstract notions or unattainable ideals; rather, it aims at an authentic and integral development, at efforts to provide dignified living conditions for everyone, at finding just responses to the needs of individuals and families, and at ensuring that God's gift of creation is respected, safeguarded and cultivated. The Venerable Paul VI described the aspirations of people today in this way: "to secure a sure food supply, cures for diseases and steady employment . . . to exercise greater personal responsibility; to do more, to learn more, and have more, in order to be more" (*Populorum Progressio*, no. 6).

Our hearts do desire something "more." Beyond greater knowledge or possessions, they want to "be" more. Development cannot be reduced to economic growth alone, often attained without a thought for the poor and the vulnerable. A better world will come about only if attention is first paid to individuals; if human promotion is integral, taking account of every dimension of the person, including the spiritual; if no one is neglected, including the poor, the sick, prisoners, the needy and the stranger (cf. Mt 25:31-46); if we can prove capable of leaving behind a throwaway culture and embracing one of encounter and acceptance.

Migrants and refugees are not pawns on the chessboard of humanity. They are children, women and men who leave or who are forced to leave their homes for various reasons, who share a legitimate desire for knowing and having, but above all for being more. The sheer number of people migrating from one continent to another, or shifting places within their own countries and geographical areas, is striking. Contemporary movements of migration represent the largest movement of individuals, if not of peoples, in history. As the Church accompanies migrants and refugees on their journey, she seeks to understand the causes of migration, but she also works to overcome its negative effects, and to maximize its positive influence on the communities of origin, transit and destination.

While encouraging the development of a better world, we cannot remain silent about the scandal of poverty in its various forms. Violence, exploitation, discrimination, marginalization, restrictive approaches to fundamental freedoms, whether of individuals or of groups: these are some of the chief elements of poverty which need to be overcome. Often these are precisely the elements which mark migratory movements, thus linking migration to poverty. Fleeing from situations of extreme poverty or persecution in the hope of a better future, or simply to save their own lives, millions of persons choose to migrate. Despite their hopes and expectations, they often encounter mistrust, rejection and exclusion, to say nothing of tragedies and disasters which offend their human dignity.

The reality of migration, given its new dimensions in our age of globalization, needs to be approached and managed in a new, equitable and effective manner; more than anything, this calls for international cooperation and a spirit of profound solidarity and compassion. Cooperation at different levels is critical, including the broad adoption of policies and rules aimed at protecting and promoting the human person. Pope Benedict XVI sketched the parameters of such policies, stating that they "should set out from close collaboration between the migrants' countries of origin and their countries of destination; they should be accompanied by adequate international norms able to coordinate different legislative systems with a view to safeguarding the needs and rights of individual migrants and their families, and at the same time, those of the host countries" (*Caritas in Veritate*, no. 62). Working together for a better world requires that countries help one another, in a spirit of willingness and trust, without raising insurmountable barriers. A good synergy can be a source of encouragement to government leaders as they confront socioeconomic imbalances and an unregulated globalization, which are among some of the causes of migration movements in which individuals are more victims than protagonists. No country can singlehandedly face the difficulties associated with this phenomenon, which is now so widespread that it affects every continent in the twofold movement of immigration and emigration.

It must also be emphasized that such cooperation begins with the efforts of each country to create better economic and social conditions at home, so that emigration will not be the only option left for those who seek peace, justice, security and full respect of their human dignity. The creation of opportunities for employment in the local economies will also avoid the separation of families and ensure that individuals and groups enjoy conditions of stability and serenity.

Finally, in considering the situation of migrants and refugees, I would point to yet another element in building a better world, namely, the elimination of prejudices and presuppositions in the approach to migration. Not infrequently, the arrival of migrants, displaced persons, asylum-seekers and refugees gives rise to suspicion and hostility. There is a fear that society will become less secure, that identity and culture will be lost, that competition for jobs will become stiffer and even that criminal activity will increase. The communications media have a role of great responsibility in this regard: it is up to them, in fact, to break down stereotypes and to offer correct information in reporting the errors of a few as well as the honesty, rectitude and goodness of the majority. A change of attitude toward migrants and refugees is needed on the part of everyone, moving away from attitudes of defensiveness and fear, indifference and marginalization—all typical of a throwaway culture—toward attitudes based on a culture of encounter, the only culture capable of building a better, more just and fraternal world. The communications media are themselves called to embrace this "conversion of attitudes" and to promote this change in the way migrants and refugees are treated.

I think of how even the Holy Family of Nazareth experienced initial rejection: Mary "gave birth to her firstborn son, and wrapped him in swaddling cloths, and laid him in a manger, because there was no place for them in the inn" (Lk 2:7). Jesus, Mary and Joseph knew what it meant to leave their own country and become migrants: threatened by Herod's lust for power, they were forced to take flight and seek refuge in Egypt (cf. Mt 2:13-14). But the maternal heart of Mary and the compassionate heart of Joseph, the Protector of the Holy Family, never doubted that God would always be with them. Through their intercession, may that same firm certainty dwell in the heart of every migrant and refugee.

The Church, responding to Christ's command to "go and make disciples of all nations," is called to be the People of God which embraces all peoples and brings to them the proclamation of the Gospel, for the face of each person bears the mark of the face of Christ! Here we find the deepest foundation of the dignity of the human person, which must always be respected and safeguarded. It is less the criteria of efficiency, productivity, social class, or ethnic or religious belonging which ground that personal dignity, so much as the fact of being created in God's own image and likeness (cf. Gen 1:26-27) and, even more so, being children of God. Every human being is a child of God! He or she bears the image of Christ! We ourselves need to see, and then to enable others to see, that migrants and refugees do not only represent a problem to be solved, but are brothers and sisters to be welcomed, respected and loved. They are an occasion that Providence gives us to help build a more just society, a more perfect democracy, a more united country, a more fraternal world and a more open and evangelical Christian community. Migration can offer possibilities for a new evangelization, open vistas for the growth of a new humanity foreshadowed in the paschal mystery: a humanity for which every foreign country is a homeland and every homeland is a foreign country.

Dear migrants and refugees! Never lose the hope that you too are facing a more secure future, that on your journey you will encounter an outstretched hand, and that you can experience fraternal solidarity and the warmth of friendship! To all of you, and to those who have devoted their lives and their efforts to helping you, I give the assurance of my prayers and I cordially impart my Apostolic Blessing.

From the Vatican, August 5, 2013

Message for the World Day of Migrants and Refugees (2015)

Church Without Frontiers, Mother to All

Dear Brothers and Sisters,

Jesus is "the evangelizer par excellence and the Gospel in person" (*Evangelii Gaudium*, no. 209). His solicitude, particularly for the most vulnerable and marginalized, invites all of us to care for the frailest and to recognize his suffering countenance, especially in the victims of new forms of poverty and slavery. The Lord says: "I was hungry and you gave me food, I was thirsty and you gave me drink, I was a stranger and you welcomed me, I was naked and you clothed me, I was sick and you visited me, I was in prison and you came to me" (Mt 25:35-36). The mission of the Church, herself a pilgrim in the world and the Mother of all, is thus to love Jesus Christ, to adore and love him, particularly in the poorest and most abandoned; among these are certainly migrants and refugees, who are trying to escape difficult living conditions and dangers of every kind. For this reason, the theme for this year's World Day of Migrants and Refugees is: *Church without frontiers, Mother to all.*

The Church opens her arms to welcome all people, without distinction or limits, in order to proclaim that "God is love" (1 Jn 4:8, 16). After his death and resurrection, Jesus entrusted to the disciples the mission of being his witnesses and proclaiming the Gospel of joy and mercy. On the day of Pentecost, the disciples left the Upper Room with courage and enthusiasm; the strength of the Holy Spirit overcame their doubts and uncertainties and enabled all to understand the disciples' preaching in their own language. From the beginning, the Church has been a mother with a heart open to the whole world, and has been without borders. This mission has continued for two thousand years. But even in the first centuries, the missionary proclamation spoke of the universal motherhood of the Church, which was then developed in the writings of the Fathers and taken up by the Second Vatican Council. The Council Fathers spoke of *Ecclesia Mater* to explain the Church's nature. She begets sons and daughters and "takes them in and embraces them with her love and in her heart" (*Lumen Gentium*, no. 14).

The Church without frontiers, Mother to all, spreads throughout the world a culture of acceptance and solidarity, in which no one is seen as useless, out of place or disposable. When living out this motherhood effectively, the Christian community nourishes, guides and indicates the way, accompanying all with patience, and drawing close to them through prayer and works of mercy.

Today this takes on a particular significance. In fact, in an age of such vast movements of migration, large numbers of people are leaving their homelands, with a suitcase full of fears and desires, to undertake a hopeful and dangerous trip in search of more humane living conditions. Often, however, such migration gives rise to suspicion and hostility, even in ecclesial communities, prior to any knowledge of the migrants' lives or their stories of persecution and destitution. In such cases, suspicion and prejudice conflict with the biblical commandment of welcoming with respect and solidarity the stranger in need.

On the other hand, we sense in our conscience the call to touch human misery, and to put into practice the commandment of love that Jesus left us when he identified himself with the stranger, with the one who suffers, with all the innocent victims of violence and exploitation. Because of the weakness of our nature, however, "we are tempted to be that kind of Christian who keeps the Lord's wounds at arm's length" (*Evangelii Gaudium*, no. 270).

The courage born of faith, hope and love enables us to reduce the distances that separate us from human misery. Jesus Christ is always waiting to be recognized in migrants and refugees, in displaced persons and in exiles, and through them he calls us to share our resources, and occasionally to give up something of our acquired riches. Pope Paul VI spoke of this when he said that "the more fortunate should renounce some of their rights so as to place their goods more generously at the service of others" (*Octogesima Adveniens*, no. 23).

The multicultural character of society today, for that matter, encourages the Church to take on new commitments of solidarity, communion and evangelization. Migration movements, in fact, call us to deepen and strengthen the values needed to guarantee peaceful coexistence between persons and cultures. Achieving mere tolerance that respects diversity and ways of sharing between different backgrounds and cultures is not sufficient. This is precisely where the Church contributes to overcoming frontiers and encouraging the "moving away from attitudes of defensiveness and fear, indifference and marginalization . . . toward attitudes based on a culture of encounter, the only culture capable of building a better, more just and fraternal world" (Message for the World Day of Migrants and Refugees 2014).

Migration movements, however, are on such a scale that only a systematic and active cooperation between States and international organizations can be capable of regulating and managing such movements effectively. For migration affects everyone, not only because of the extent of the phenomenon, but also because of "the social, economic, political, cultural and religious problems it raises, and the dramatic challenges it poses to nations and the international community" (*Caritas in Veritate*, no. 62).

At the international level, frequent debates take place regarding the appropriateness, methods and required norms to deal with the phenomenon of migration. There are agencies and organizations on the international, national and local level which work strenuously to serve those seeking a better life through migration. Notwithstanding their generous and laudable efforts, a more decisive and constructive action is required, one which relies on a universal network of cooperation, based on safeguarding the dignity and centrality of every human person. This will lead to greater effectiveness in the fight against the shameful and criminal trafficking of human beings, the violation of fundamental rights, and all forms of violence, oppression and enslavement. Working together, however, requires reciprocity, joint-action, openness and trust, in the knowledge that "no country can singlehandedly face the difficulties associated with this phenomenon, which is now so widespread that it affects every continent in the twofold movement of immigration and emigration" (Message for the World Day of Migrants and Refugees 2014).

It is necessary to respond to the globalization of migration with the globalization of charity and cooperation, in such a way as to make the conditions of migrants more humane. At the same time, greater efforts are needed to guarantee the easing of conditions, often brought about by war or famine, which compel whole peoples to leave their native countries.

Solidarity with migrants and refugees must be accompanied by the courage and creativity necessary to develop, on a world-wide level, a more just and equitable financial and economic order, as well as an increasing commitment to peace, the indispensable condition for all authentic progress.

Dear migrants and refugees! You have a special place in the heart of the Church, and you help her to enlarge her heart and to manifest her motherhood toward the entire human family. Do not lose your faith and hope! Let us think of the Holy Family during the flight in Egypt: Just as the maternal heart of the Blessed Virgin and the kind heart of Saint Joseph kept alive the confidence that God would never abandon them, so in you may the same hope in the Lord never be wanting. I entrust you to their protection and I cordially impart to all of you my Apostolic Blessing.

From the Vatican, September 3, 2014

Message for the World Day of Migrants and Refugees

January 17, 2016

"Migrants and Refugees Challenge Us. The Response of the Gospel of Mercy"

Dear Brothers and Sisters,

In the Bull of indiction of the Extraordinary Jubilee of Mercy I noted that "at times we are called to gaze even more attentively on mercy so that we may become a more effective sign of the Father's action in our lives" (*Misericordiae Vultus*, no. 3). God's love is meant to reach out to each and every person. Those who welcome the Father's embrace, for their part, become so many other open arms and embraces, enabling every person to feel loved like a child and "at home" as part of the one human family. God's fatherly care extends to everyone, like the care of a shepherd for his flock, but it is particularly concerned for the needs of the sheep who are wounded, weary or ill. Jesus told us that the Father stoops to help those overcome by physical or moral poverty; the more serious their condition, the more powerfully is his divine mercy revealed.

In our time, migration is growing worldwide. Refugees and people fleeing from their homes challenge individuals and communities, and their traditional ways of life; at times they upset the cultural and social horizons which they encounter. Increasingly, the victims of violence and poverty, leaving their homelands, are exploited by human traffickers during their journey toward the dream of a better future. If they survive the abuses and hardships of the journey, they then have to face latent suspicions and fear. In the end, they frequently encounter a lack of clear and practical policies regulating the acceptance of migrants and providing for short or long-term programs of integration respectful of the rights and duties of all. Today, more than in the past, the Gospel of mercy troubles our consciences, prevents us from taking the suffering of others for granted, and points out way of responding which, grounded in the theological virtues of faith, hope and charity, find practical expression in works of spiritual and corporal mercy.

In the light of these facts, I have chosen as the theme of the 2016 World Day of Migrants and Refugees: *Migrants and Refugees Challenge Us. The Response of the Gospel of Mercy.* Migration movements are now a structural reality, and our primary issue must be to deal with the present emergency phase by providing programs which address the causes of migration and the changes it entails, including its effect on the makeup of societies and peoples. The tragic stories of millions of men and women daily confront the international community as a result of the outbreak of unacceptable humanitarian crises in different parts of the world. Indifference and silence lead to complicity whenever we stand by as people are dying of suffocation, starvation, violence and shipwreck. Whether large or small in scale, these are always tragedies, even when a single human life is lost.

Migrants are our brothers and sisters in search of a better life, far away from poverty, hunger, exploitation and the unjust distribution of the planet's resources which are meant to be equitably shared by all. Don't we all want a better, more decent and prosperous life to share with our loved ones?

At this moment in human history, marked by great movements of migration, identity is not a secondary issue. Those who migrate are forced to change some of their most distinctive characteristics and, whether they like or not, even those who welcome them are also forced to change. How can we experience these changes not as obstacles to genuine development, [but] rather as opportunities for genuine human, social and spiritual growth, a growth which respects and promotes those values which make us ever more humane and help us to live a balanced relationship with God, others and creation?

The presence of migrants and refugees seriously challenges the various societies which accept them. Those societies are faced with new situations which could create serious hardship unless they are suitably motivated, managed and regulated. How can we ensure that integration will become mutual enrichment, open up positive perspectives to communities, and prevent the danger of discrimination, racism, extreme nationalism or xenophobia?

Biblical revelation urges us to welcome the stranger; it tells us that in so doing, we open our doors to God, and that in the faces of others we see the face of Christ himself. Many institutions, associations, movements and groups, diocesan, national and international organizations are experiencing the wonder and joy of the feast of encounter, sharing and solidarity. They have heard the voice of Jesus Christ: "Behold, I stand at the door and knock" (Rev 3:20). Yet there continue to be debates about the conditions and limits to be set for the reception of migrants, not only on the level of national policies, but also in some parish communities whose traditional tranquility seems to be threatened.

Faced with these issues, how can the Church fail to be inspired by the example and words of Jesus Christ? The answer of the Gospel is mercy.

In the first place, mercy is a gift of God the Father who is revealed in the Son. God's mercy gives rise to joyful gratitude for the hope which opens up before us in the mystery of our redemption by Christ's blood. Mercy nourishes and strengthens solidarity toward others as a necessary response to God's gracious love, "which has been poured into our hearts through the Holy Spirit" (Rom 5:5). Each of us is responsible for his or her neighbor: we are our brothers' and sisters' keepers, wherever they live. Concern for fostering good relationships with others and the ability to overcome prejudice and fear are essential ingredients for promoting the culture of encounter, in which we are not only prepared to give, but also to receive from others. Hospitality, in fact, grows from both giving and receiving.

From this perspective, it is important to view migrants not only on the basis of their status as regular or irregular, but above all as people whose dignity is to be protected and who are capable of contributing to progress and the general welfare. This is especially the case when they responsibly assume their obligations toward those who receive them, gratefully respecting the material and spiritual heritage of the host country, obeying its laws and helping with its needs. Migrations cannot be reduced merely to their political and legislative aspects, their economic implications and the concrete coexistence of various cultures in one territory. All these complement the defense and promotion of the human person, the culture of encounter, and the unity of peoples, where the Gospel of mercy inspires and encourages ways of renewing and transforming the whole of humanity.

The Church stands at the side of all who work to defend each person's right to live with dignity, first and foremost by exercising the right not to emigrate and to contribute to the development of one's country of origin. This process should include, from the outset, the need to assist the countries which migrants and refugees leave. This will demonstrate that solidarity, cooperation, international interdependence and the equitable distribution of the earth's goods are essential for more decisive efforts, especially in areas where migration movements begin, to eliminate those imbalances which lead people, individually or collectively, to abandon their own natural and cultural environment. In any case, it is necessary to avert, if possible at the earliest stages, the flight of refugees and departures as a result of poverty, violence and persecution.

Public opinion also needs to be correctly formed, not least to prevent unwarranted fears and speculations detrimental to migrants.

No one can claim to be indifferent in the face of new forms of slavery imposed by criminal organizations which buy and sell men, women and children as forced laborers in construction, agriculture, fishing or in other markets. How many minors are still forced to fight in militias as child soldiers! How many people are victims of organ trafficking, forced begging and sexual exploitation! Today's refugees are fleeing from these aberrant crimes, and they appeal to the Church and the human community to ensure that, in the outstretched hand of those who receive them, they can see the face of the Lord, "the Father of mercies and God of all consolation" (2 Cor 1:3).

Dear brothers and sisters, migrants and refugees! At the heart of the Gospel of mercy the encounter and acceptance by others are intertwined with the encounter and acceptance of God himself. Welcoming others means welcoming God in person! Do not let yourselves be robbed of the hope and joy of life born of your experience of God's mercy, as manifested in the people you meet on your journey! I entrust you to the Virgin Mary, Mother of migrants and refugees, and to Saint Joseph, who experienced the bitterness of emigration to Egypt. To their intercession I also commend those who invest so much energy, time and resources to the pastoral and social care of migrants. To all I cordially impart my Apostolic Blessing.

From the Vatican, September 12, 2015
Memorial of the Holy Name of Mary

Message for the World Day of Migrants and Refugees

January 15, 2017

"Child Migrants, the Vulnerable and the Voiceless"

Dear Brothers and Sisters,

"Whoever receives one such child in my name receives me; and whoever receives me, receives not me but him who sent me" (Mk 9:37; cf. Mt 18:5; Lk 9:48; Jn 13:20). With these words, the Evangelists remind the Christian community of Jesus' teaching, which both inspires and challenges. This phrase traces the sure path which leads to God; it begins with the smallest and, through the grace of our Savior, it grows into the practice of welcoming others. To be welcoming is a necessary condition for making this journey a concrete reality: God made himself one of us. In Jesus God became a child, and the openness of faith to God, which nourishes hope, is expressed in loving proximity to the smallest and the weakest. Charity, faith and hope are all actively present in the spiritual and corporal works of mercy, as we have rediscovered during the recent Extraordinary Jubilee.

But the Evangelists reflect also on the responsibility of the one who works against mercy: "Whoever causes one of these little ones who believe in me to sin: it is better for him to have a great millstone fastened round his neck and be drowned in the depth of the sea" (Mt 18:6; cf. Mk 9:42; Lk 17:2). How can we ignore this severe warning when we see the exploitation carried out by unscrupulous people? Such exploitation harms young girls and boys who are led into prostitution or into the mire of pornography; who are enslaved as child laborers or soldiers; who are caught up in drug trafficking and other forms of criminality; who are forced to flee from conflict and persecution, risking isolation and abandonment.

For this reason, on the occasion of the annual World Day of Migrants and Refugees, I feel compelled to draw attention to the reality of child migrants, especially the ones who are alone. In doing so I ask everyone to take care of the young, who in a threefold way are defenseless: they are children, they are foreigners, and they have no means to protect themselves. I ask everyone to help those who, for various reasons, are forced to live far from their homeland and are separated from their families.

Migration today is not a phenomenon limited to some areas of the planet. It affects all continents and is growing into a tragic situation of global proportions. Not only does this concern those looking for dignified work or better living conditions, but also men and women, the elderly and children, who are forced to leave their homes in the hope of finding safety, peace and security. Children are the first among those to pay the heavy toll of emigration, almost always caused by violence, poverty, environmental conditions, as well as the negative aspects of globalization. The unrestrained competition for quick and easy profit brings with it the cultivation of perverse scourges such as child trafficking, the exploitation and abuse of minors and, generally, the depriving of rights intrinsic to childhood as sanctioned by the International Convention on the Rights of the Child.

Childhood, given its fragile nature, has unique and inalienable needs. Above all else, there is the right to a healthy and secure family environment, where a child can grow under the guidance and example of a father and a mother; then there is the right and duty to receive adequate education, primarily in the family and also in the school, where children can grow as persons and agents of their own future and the future of their respective countries. Indeed, in many areas of the world, reading, writing and the most basic arithmetic is still the privilege of only a few. All children, furthermore, have the right to recreation; in a word, they have the right to be children.

And yet among migrants, children constitute the most vulnerable group, because as they face the life ahead of them, they are invisible and voiceless: their precarious situation deprives them of documentation, hiding them from the world's eyes; the absence of adults to accompany them prevents their voices from being raised and heard. In this way, migrant children easily end up at the lowest levels of human degradation, where illegality and violence destroy the future of too many innocents, while the network of child abuse is difficult to break up.

How should we respond to this reality?

Firstly, we need to become aware that the phenomenon of migration is not unrelated to salvation history, but rather a part of that history. One of God's commandments is connected to it: "You shall not wrong a stranger or oppress him, for you were strangers in the land of Egypt" (Ex 22:21); "Love the sojourner therefore; for you were sojourners in the land of Egypt" (Dt 10:19). This phenomenon constitutes *a sign of the times*, a sign which speaks of the providential work of God in history and in the human community, with a view to universal communion. While appreciating the issues, and often the suffering and tragedy of migration, as too the difficulties connected with the demands of offering a dignified welcome to these persons, the Church nevertheless encourages us to recognize God's plan. She invites us to do this precisely amidst this phenomenon, with the certainty that no one is a stranger in the Christian community, which embraces "every nation, tribe, people and tongue" (Rev 7:9). Each person is precious; persons are more important than things, and the worth of an institution is measured by the way it treats the life and dignity of human beings, particularly when they are vulnerable, as in the case of child migrants.

Furthermore, we need to work toward *protection, integration* and *long-term solutions.*

We are primarily concerned with adopting every possible measure to guarantee the *protection and safety* of child migrants, because "these boys and girls often end up on the street abandoned to themselves and prey to unscrupulous exploiters who often transform them into the object of physical, moral and sexual violence" (Benedict XVI, *Message for the World Day of Migrants and Refugees,* 2008).

Moreover, the dividing line between migration and trafficking can at times be very subtle. There are many factors which contribute to making migrants vulnerable, especially if they are children: poverty and the lack of means to survive—to which are added unrealistic expectations generated by the media; the low level of literacy; ignorance of the law, of the culture and frequently of the language of host countries. All of this renders children physically and psychologically dependent. But the most powerful force driving the exploitation and abuse of children is demand. If more rigorous and effective action is not taken against those who profit from such abuse, we will not be able to stop the multiple forms of slavery where children are the victims.

It is necessary, therefore, for immigrants to cooperate ever more closely with the communities that welcome them, for the good of their own children. We are deeply grateful to organizations and institutions, both ecclesial and civil, that commit time and resources to protect minors from various forms of abuse. It is important that evermore effective and incisive cooperation be implemented, based not only on the exchange of information, but also on the reinforcement of networks capable of assuring timely and specific intervention; and this, without underestimating the strength that ecclesial communities reveal especially when they are united in prayer and fraternal communion.

Secondly, we need to work for the *integration* of children and youngsters who are migrants. They depend totally on the adult community. Very often the scarcity of financial resources prevents the adoption of adequate policies aimed at assistance and inclusion. As a result, instead of favoring the social integration of child migrants, or programs for safe and assisted repatriation, there is simply an attempt to curb the entrance of migrants, which in turn fosters illegal networks; or else immigrants are repatriated to their country of origin without any concern for their "best interests."

The condition of child migrants is worsened when their status is not regularized or when they are recruited by criminal organizations. In such cases they are usually sent to detention centers. It is not unusual for them to be arrested, and because they have no money to pay the fine or for the return journey, they can be incarcerated for long periods, exposed to various kinds of abuse and violence. In these instances, the right of states to control migratory movement and to protect the common good of the nation must be seen in conjunction with the duty to resolve and regularize the situation of child migrants, fully respecting their dignity and seeking to meet their needs when they are alone, but also the needs of their parents, for the good of the entire family.

Of fundamental importance is the adoption of adequate national procedures and mutually agreed plans of cooperation between countries of origin and of destination, with the intention of eliminating the causes of the forced emigration of minors.

Thirdly, to all I address a heartfelt appeal that *long-term solutions* be sought and adopted. Since this is a complex phenomenon, the question of child migrants must be tackled at its source. Wars, human rights violations, corruption, poverty, environmental imbalance and disasters, are all causes of this problem. Children are the first to suffer, at times suffering torture and other physical violence, in addition to moral and psychological aggression, which almost always leave indelible scars.

It is absolutely necessary, therefore, to deal with the causes which trigger migrations in the countries of origin. This requires, as a first step, the commitment of the whole international community to eliminate the conflicts and violence that force people to flee. Furthermore, far-sighted perspectives are called for, capable of offering adequate programs for areas struck by the worst injustice and instability, in order that access to authentic development can be guaranteed for all. This development should promote the good of boys and girls, who are humanity's hope.

Lastly, I wish to address a word to you, who walk alongside migrant children and young people: they need your precious help. The Church too needs you and supports you in the generous service you offer. Do not tire of courageously living the Gospel, which calls you to recognize and welcome the Lord Jesus among the smallest and most vulnerable.

I entrust all child migrants, their families, their communities, and you who are close to them, to the protection of the Holy Family of Nazareth; may they watch over and accompany each one on their journey. With my prayers, I gladly impart my Apostolic Blessing.

From the Vatican, September 8, 2016

Address to the National Directors of Pastoral Care for Migrants, Catholic Bishops' Conferences of Europe

Clementine Hall

September 22, 2017

Dear Brothers and Sisters,

I am pleased to welcome you here on the occasion of your meeting, and I thank the Cardinal President for his kind words on your behalf. I am very grateful to all of you for the great effort you have made in recent years to help the many migrants and refugees who knock at Europe's doors in search of a place of safety and a more dignified life.

The complex and varied phenomenon of continued migration has overwhelmed existing immigration policies and measures for the protection of migrants ratified by international agreements. In the face of this crisis, the Church is committed to remain faithful to her mission "to love Jesus Christ, to adore and love him, particularly in the poorest and most abandoned" (*Message for the World Day of Migrants and Refugees*, 2015).

The Church's maternal love for these, our brothers and sisters, must be concretely shown at every stage of their journey, from start to finish, in such a manner that ecclesial communities and organizations at every step of the way take an active part in this one mission, each to the best of its ability. Seeing and serving the Lord in these members of his "pilgrim people" is a responsibility that unites all the particular Churches in the effort to provide a constant, coordinated and effective outreach.

Dear friends, I cannot fail to express my concern about manifestations of intolerance, discrimination and xenophobia that have appeared in various parts of Europe. Often this reaction is motivated by mistrust and fear of the other, the foreigner, those who are different. I am even more worried about the disturbing fact that our Catholic communities in Europe are not exempt from these defensive and negative reactions, supposedly justified by a vague moral obligation to preserve an established religious and cultural identity. The Church has spread to all continents thanks to the "migration" of missionaries convinced of the universality of the saving message of Jesus Christ, meant for men and women of every culture. Throughout the history of the Church, there have been temptations to exclusivity and cultural rigidity, but the Holy Spirit has always helped overcome them by ensuring constant openness to others, viewed as a positive opportunity for growth and enrichment.

I am sure that the Holy Spirit also helps us today to maintain a confident attitude of openness, capable of surmounting every barrier and breaking down every wall.

In listening attentively to the particular Churches in Europe, I sense a deep unease about the massive influx of migrants and refugees. That unease needs to be acknowledged and appreciated in the light of this moment of history, marked by an economic crisis that has left deep wounds. It has also been aggravated by the sheer size and makeup of the continuing waves of migrants, the general unpreparedness of the countries that receive them, and by often inadequate national and community policies. But the unease is also indicative of the limits of the process of European unification, and points up the obstacles hindering the concrete application of universal human rights and the expression of that integral humanism which is among the finest fruits of European civilization. For Christians all these factors must be interpreted, in opposition to a self-enclosed and secularist mentality, in the light of the unique, God-given dignity of each human person.

From a distinctively ecclesiological perspective, the arrival of great numbers of our brothers and sisters in the faith offers the Churches in Europe yet another opportunity to embody fully its catholicity, which, as we profess in the creed each Sunday, is a fundamental mark of the

Church. In recent years, many dioceses in Europe have already found themselves enriched by the presence of Catholic immigrants who have brought with them their devotions, and their liturgical and apostolic enthusiasm.

From a missionary perspective, the current influx of migrants can be seen as a new "frontier" for mission, a privileged opportunity to proclaim Jesus Christ and the Gospel message at home, and to bear concrete witness to the Christian faith in a spirit of charity and profound esteem for other religious communities. The encounter with migrants and refugees of other denominations and religions represents a fertile ground for the growth of open and enriching ecumenical and interreligious dialogue.

In my Message for the 2018 World Day of Migrants and Refugees, I suggested that our pastoral response to the challenges of contemporary movements of migration can be expressed by four verbs: *to welcome*, *to protect*, *to promote and to integrate*. *Welcoming* means expanding legal and secure programs of reception for those who arrive, as well as offering suitable and dignified accommodations that guarantee their personal safety and access to basic services. *Protecting* involves offering trustworthy and verified information to migrants and refugees prior to their departure, defending their basic rights independent of their legal status, and watching over the most vulnerable, the young children. *Promoting* essentially means ensuring the conditions for the integral human development of all, migrants and natives alike. *Integrating* entails expanding opportunities for intercultural encounter, fostering mutual enrichment and promoting active citizenship.

In the same Message, I also emphasized the importance of the global agreements that States have committed themselves to draft and approve by the end of 2018. The Section for Migrants and Refugees of the Dicastery for Promoting Integral Human Development has prepared twenty action points that various local Churches can utilize, integrate and develop in their pastoral outreach. The points are based on the "best practices" that characterize the Church's tangible response to the needs of migrants and refugees. These points can also prove helpful for discussions that various ecclesial institutions can have with government authorities in view of these global agreements. I would encourage you to familiarize yourselves with these points and to promote them through your episcopal conferences.

Those action points also make up a "paradigm" of the four verbs I mentioned above, a paradigm that can serve as a criterion and yardstick for the pastoral practices of the local Churches and an aid in updating and improving them. May the spirit of communion in reflection and action be a source of strength for all of you, since challenges faced alone always appear more daunting. May your interventions continue to be timely and prophetic, and, above all, the fruit of actions consistent with, and inspired by, the principles of Christian doctrine.

Once again, I express my appreciation of your generous commitment to the complex and urgent work of offering pastoral care to migrants. I assure you of my prayers for your intentions, and I ask you, please, not to forget to pray for me.

Message for the Celebration of the World Day of Peace

January 1, 2018

Migrants and Refugees: Men and Women in Search of Peace

1. Heartfelt good wishes for peace

Peace to all people and to all nations on earth! Peace, which the angels proclaimed to the shepherds on Christmas night,[1] is a profound aspiration for everyone, for each individual and all peoples, and especially for those who most keenly suffer its absence. Among these whom I constantly keep in my thoughts and prayers, I would once again mention the over 250 million migrants worldwide, of whom 22.5 million are refugees. Pope Benedict XVI, my beloved predecessor, spoke of them as "men and women, children, young and elderly people, who are searching for somewhere to live in peace."[2] In order to find that peace, they are willing to risk their lives on a journey that is often long and perilous, to endure hardships and suffering, and to encounter fences and walls built to keep them far from their goal.

In a spirit of compassion, let us embrace all those fleeing from war and hunger, or forced by discrimination, persecution, poverty and environmental degradation to leave their homelands.

We know that it is not enough to open our hearts to the suffering of others. Much more remains to be done before our brothers and sisters can once again live peacefully in a safe home. Welcoming others requires concrete commitment, a network of assistance and goodwill, vigilant and sympathetic attention, the responsible management of new and complex situations that at times compound numerous existing problems, to say nothing of resources, which are always limited. By practicing the virtue of prudence, government leaders should take practical measures to welcome, promote, protect, integrate and, "within the limits allowed by a correct understanding of the common good, to permit [them] to become part of a new society."[3] Leaders have a clear responsibility toward their own communities, whose legitimate rights and harmonious development they must ensure, lest they become like the rash builder who miscalculated and failed to complete the tower he had begun to construct.[4]

2. Why so many refugees and migrants?

As he looked to the Great Jubilee marking the passage of two thousand years since the proclamation of peace by the angels in Bethlehem, Saint John Paul II pointed to the increased numbers of displaced persons as one of the consequences of the "endless and horrifying sequence of wars, conflicts, genocides and ethnic cleansings"[5] that had characterized the twentieth century. To this date, the new century has registered no real breakthrough: armed conflicts and other forms of organized violence continue to trigger the movement of peoples within national borders and beyond.

Yet people migrate for other reasons as well, principally because they "desire a better life, and not infrequently try to leave behind the 'hopelessness' of an unpromising future."[6] They set out to join their families or to seek professional or educational opportunities, for those who cannot enjoy these rights do not live in peace. Furthermore, as I noted in the Encyclical *Laudato Si'*, there has been "a tragic rise in the number of migrants seeking to flee from the growing poverty caused by environmental degradation."[7]

Most people migrate through regular channels. Some, however, take different routes, mainly out of desperation, when their own countries offer neither safety nor opportunity, and every legal pathway appears impractical, blocked or too slow.

Many destination countries have seen the spread of rhetoric decrying the risks posed to national security or the high cost of welcoming new arrivals, and thus demeaning the human dignity due to all as sons and daughters of God. Those who, for what may be political reasons, foment fear of migrants instead of building peace are sowing violence, racial discrimination and xenophobia, which are matters of great concern for all those concerned for the safety of every human being.[8]

All indicators available to the international community suggest that global migration will continue for the future. Some consider this a threat. For my part, I ask you to view it with confidence as an opportunity to build peace.

3. With a contemplative gaze

The wisdom of faith fosters a contemplative gaze that recognizes that all of us "belong to one family, migrants and the local populations that welcome them, and all have the same right to enjoy the goods of the earth, whose destination is universal, as the social doctrine of the Church teaches. It is here that solidarity and sharing are founded."[9] These words evoke the biblical image of the new Jerusalem. The book of the prophet Isaiah (chapter 60) and that of Revelation (chapter 21) describe the city with its gates always open to people of every nation, who marvel at it and fill it with riches. Peace is the sovereign that guides it and justice the principle that governs coexistence within it.

We must also turn this contemplative gaze to the cities where we live, "a gaze of faith which sees God dwelling in their houses, in their streets and squares, [...] fostering solidarity, fraternity, and the desire for goodness, truth and justice"[10]—in other words, fulfilling the promise of peace.

When we turn that gaze to migrants and refugees, we discover that they do not arrive empty-handed. They bring their courage, skills, energy and aspirations, as well as the treasures of their own cultures; and in this way, they enrich the lives of the nations that receive them. We also come to see the creativity, tenacity and spirit of sacrifice of the countless individuals, families and communities around the world who open their doors and hearts to migrants and refugees, even where resources are scarce.

A contemplative gaze should also guide the discernment of those responsible for the public good, and encourage them to pursue policies of welcome, "within the limits allowed by a correct understanding of the common good"[11]—bearing in mind, that is, the needs of all members of the human family and the welfare of each.

Those who see things in this way will be able to recognize the seeds of peace that are already sprouting and nurture their growth. Our cities, often divided and polarized by conflicts regarding the presence of migrants and refugees, will thus turn into workshops of peace.

4. Four mileposts for action

Offering asylum seekers, refugees, migrants and victims of human trafficking an opportunity to find the peace they seek requires a strategy combining four actions: welcoming, protecting, promoting and integrating.[12]

"Welcoming" calls for expanding legal pathways for entry and no longer pushing migrants and displaced people toward countries where they face persecution and violence. It also demands balancing our concerns about national security with concern for fundamental human rights. Scripture reminds us: "Do not forget to show hospitality to strangers, for by so doing some people have shown hospitality to angels without knowing it."[13]

"Protecting" has to do with our duty to recognize and defend the inviolable dignity of those who flee real dangers in search of asylum and security, and to prevent their being exploited. I think in particular of women and children who find themselves in situations that expose them to risks and abuses that can even amount to enslavement. God does not discriminate: "The Lord watches over the foreigner and sustains the orphan and the widow."[14]

"Promoting" entails supporting the integral human development of migrants and refugees. Among many possible means of doing so, I would stress the importance of ensuring access to all levels of education for children and young people. This will enable them not only to cultivate and realize their potential, but also better equip them to encounter others and to foster a spirit of dialogue rather than rejection or confrontation. The Bible teaches that God "loves the foreigner residing among you, giving them food and clothing. And you are to love those who are foreigners, for you yourselves were foreigners in Egypt."[15]

"Integrating," lastly, means allowing refugees and migrants to participate fully in the life of the society that welcomes them, as part of a process of mutual enrichment and fruitful cooperation in service of the integral human development of the local community. Saint Paul expresses it in these words: "You are no longer foreigners and strangers, but fellow citizens with God's people."[16]

5. A proposal for two international compacts

It is my heartfelt hope this spirit will guide the process that in the course of 2018 will lead the United Nations to draft and approve two Global Compacts, one for safe, orderly and regular migration and the other for refugees. As shared agreements at a global level, these compacts will provide a framework for policy proposals and practical measures. For this reason, they need to be inspired by compassion, foresight and courage, so as to take advantage of every opportunity to advance the peace-building process. Only in this way can the realism required of international politics avoid surrendering to cynicism and to the globalization of indifference.

Dialogue and coordination are a necessity and a specific duty for the international community. Beyond national borders, higher numbers of refugees may be welcomed—or better welcomed—also by less wealthy countries, if international cooperation guarantees them the necessary funding.

The Migrants and Refugees Section of the Dicastery for Promoting Integral Human Development has published a set of twenty action points that provide concrete leads for implementing these four verbs in public policy and in the attitudes and activities of Christian communities.[17] The aim of this and other contributions is to express the interest of the Catholic Church in the process leading to the adoption of the two U.N. Global Compacts. This interest is the sign of a more general pastoral concern that goes back to the very origins of the Church and has continued in her many works up to the present time.

6. For our common home

Let us draw inspiration from the words of Saint John Paul II: "If the 'dream' of a peaceful world is shared by all, if the refugees' and migrants' contribution is properly evaluated, then humanity can become more and more a universal family and our earth a true 'common home'"[18] Throughout history, many have believed in this "dream," and their achievements are a testament to the fact that it is no mere utopia.

Among these, we remember Saint Frances Xavier Cabrini in this year that marks the hundredth anniversary of her death. On this thirteenth day of November, many ecclesial communities celebrate her memory. This remarkable woman, who devoted her life to the service of migrants and became their patron saint, taught us to welcome, protect, promote and integrate our brothers and sisters. Through her intercession, may the Lord enable all of us to experience that "a harvest of righteousness is sown in peace by those who make peace."[19]

From the Vatican, November 13, 2017
Memorial of Saint Frances Xavier Cabrini, Patroness
of Migrants

Notes

1   Luke 2:14.

2   Angelus, January 15, 2012.

3   John XXIII, Encyclical Letter *Pacem in Terris*, 106.

4   Luke 14:28-30.

5   Message for the 2000 World Day of Peace, 3.

6   Benedict XVI, Message for the 2013 World Day of Migrants and Refugees.

7   No. 25.

8   Cf. Address to the National Directors of Pastoral Care for Migrants of the Catholic Bishops' Conferences of Europe, September 22, 2017.

9   Benedict XVI, Message for the 2011 World Day of Migrants and Refugees.

10 Apostolic Exhortation *Evangelii Gaudium*, 71.

11 John XXIII, Encyclical Letter *Pacem in Terris*, 106.

12 Message for the 2018 World Day of Migrants and Refugees.

13 Hebrews 13:2.

14 Psalm 146:9.

15 Deuteronomy 10:18-19.

16 Ephesians 2:19.

17 "20 Pastoral Action Points" and "20 Action Points for the Global Compacts," Migrants and Refugees Section, Rome, 2017. See also Document UN A/72/528.

18 Message for the World Day of Migrants and Refugees 2004, 6.

19 James 3:18.

Message for the World Day of Migrants and Refugees

January 14, 2018

"Welcoming, protecting, promoting and integrating migrants and refugees"

Dear brothers and sisters!

"You shall treat the stranger who sojourns with you as the native among you, and you shall love him as yourself, for you were strangers in the land of Egypt: I am the Lord your God" (Lv 19:34).

Throughout the first years of my pontificate, I have repeatedly expressed my particular concern for the lamentable situation of many migrants and refugees fleeing from war, persecution, natural disasters and poverty. This situation is undoubtedly a "sign of the times" which I have tried to interpret, with the help of the Holy Spirit, ever since my visit to Lampedusa on July 8, 2013. When I instituted the new Dicastery for Promoting Integral Human Development, I wanted a particular section—under my personal direction for the time being to express the Church's concern for migrants, displaced people, refugees and victims of human trafficking.

Every stranger who knocks at our door is an opportunity for an encounter with Jesus Christ, who identifies with the welcomed and rejected strangers of every age (Mt 25:35-43). The Lord entrusts to the Church's motherly love every person forced to leave their homeland in search of a better future.[1] This solidarity must be concretely expressed at every stage of the migratory experience—from departure through journey to arrival and return. This is a great responsibility, which the Church intends to share with all believers and men and women of good will, who are called to respond to the many challenges of contemporary migration with generosity, promptness, wisdom and foresight, each according to their own abilities.

In this regard, I wish to reaffirm that "our shared response may be articulated by four verbs: *to welcome, to protect, to promote* and *to integrate.*"[2]

Considering the current situation, *welcoming* means, above all, offering broader options for migrants and refugees to enter destination countries safely and legally. This calls for a concrete commitment to increase and simplify the process for granting humanitarian visas and for reunifying families. At the same time, I hope that a greater number of countries will adopt private and community sponsorship programs, and open humanitarian corridors for particularly vulnerable refugees. Furthermore, special temporary visas should be granted to people fleeing conflicts in neighboring countries. Collective and arbitrary expulsions of migrants and refugees are not suitable solutions, particularly where people are returned to countries which cannot guarantee respect for human dignity and fundamental rights.[3] Once again, I want to emphasize the importance of offering migrants and refugees adequate and dignified initial accommodation. "More widespread programs of welcome, already initiated in different places, seem to favor a personal encounter and allow for greater quality of service and increased guarantees of success."[4] The principle of the centrality of the human person, firmly stated by my beloved Predecessor, Benedict XVI,[5] obliges us to always prioritize personal safety over national security. It is necessary, therefore, to ensure that agents in charge of border control are properly trained. The situation of migrants, asylum seekers and refugees requires that they be guaranteed personal safety and access to basic services. For the sake of the fundamental dignity of every human person, we must strive to find alternative solutions to detention for those who enter a country without authorization.[6]

The second verb—*protecting*—may be understood as a series of steps intended to defend the rights and dignity of migrants and refugees, independent of their legal status.[7] Such protection begins in the country of origin, and consists in offering reliable and verified information before departure, and in providing safety from illegal recruitment practices.[8] This must be ongoing, as far as possible, in the country of migration, guaranteeing them adequate consular assistance, the right to personally retain their identity documents at all times, fair access to justice, the possibility of opening a personal bank account, and a minimum sufficient to live on. When duly recognized and valued, the potential and skills of migrants, asylum seekers and refugees are a true resource for the communities that welcome them.[9] This is why I hope that, in countries of arrival, migrants may be offered freedom of movement, work opportunities, and access to means of communication, out of respect for their dignity. For those who decide to return to their homeland, I want to emphasize the need to develop social and professional reintegration programs. The *International Convention on the Rights of the Child* provides a universal legal basis for the protection of underage migrants. They must be spared any form of detention related to migratory status, and must be guaranteed regular access to primary and secondary education. Equally, when they come of age they must be guaranteed the right to remain and to enjoy the possibility of continuing their studies. Temporary custody or foster programs should be provided for unaccompanied minors and minors separated from their families.[10] The universal right to a nationality should be recognized and duly certified for all children at birth. The statelessness which migrants and refugees sometimes fall into can easily be avoided with the adoption of "nationality legislation that is in conformity with the fundamental principles of international law."[11] Migratory status should not limit access to national healthcare and pension plans, nor affect the transfer of their contributions if repatriated.

Promoting essentially means a determined effort to ensure that all migrants and refugees—as well as the communities which welcome—are empowered to achieve their potential as human beings, in all the dimensions which constitute the humanity intended by the Creator.[12] Among these, we must recognize the true value of the religious dimension, ensuring to all foreigners in any country the freedom of religious belief and practice. Many migrants and refugees have abilities which must be appropriately recognized and valued. Since "work, by its nature, is meant to unite peoples,"[13] I encourage a determined effort to promote the social and professional inclusion of migrants and refugees, guaranteeing for all—including those seeking asylum—the possibility of employment, language instruction and active citizenship, together with sufficient information provided in their mother tongue. In the case of underage migrants, their involvement in labor must be regulated to prevent exploitation and risks to their normal growth and development. In 2006, Benedict XVI highlighted how, in the context of migration, the family is "a place and resource of the culture of life and a factor for the integration of values."[14] The family's integrity must always be promoted, supporting family reunifications—including grandparents, grandchildren and siblings—independent of financial requirements. Migrants, asylum seekers and refugees with disabilities must be granted greater assistance and support. While I recognize the praiseworthy efforts, thus far, of many countries, in terms of international cooperation and humanitarian aid, I hope that the offering of this assistance will take into account the needs (such as medical and social assistance, as well as education) of developing countries which receive a significant influx of migrants and refugees. I also hope that local communities which are vulnerable and facing material hardship, will be included among aid beneficiaries.[15]

The final verb—*integrating*—concerns the opportunities for intercultural enrichment brought about by the presence of migrants and refugees. Integration is not "an assimilation that leads migrants to suppress or to forget their own cultural identity. Rather, contact with others leads to discovering their 'secret,' to being open to them in order to welcome their valid aspects and thus contribute to knowing each one better. This is a lengthy process that aims to shape societies and cultures, making them more and more a reflection of the multi-faceted gifts of God to human beings."[16] This process can be accelerated by granting citizenship free of financial or linguistic requirements, and by offering the possibility of special legalization to migrants who can claim a long period of residence in the country of arrival. I reiterate the need to foster a culture of encounter in every way possible—by increasing opportunities for intercultural exchange, documenting and disseminating best practices of integration, and developing programs to prepare local communities for integration processes. I wish to stress the special case of people forced to abandon their country of arrival due to a humanitarian crisis. These people must be ensured adequate assistance for repatriation and effective reintegration programs in their home countries.

In line with her pastoral tradition, the Church is ready to commit herself to realizing all the initiatives proposed above. Yet in order to achieve the desired outcome, the contribution of political communities and civil societies is indispensable, each according to their own responsibilities.

At the United Nations Summit held in New York on September 19, 2016, world leaders clearly expressed their desire to take decisive action in support of migrants and refugees to save their lives and protect their rights, sharing this responsibility on a global level. To this end, the states committed themselves to drafting and approving, before the end of 2018, two Global Compacts, one for refugees and the other for migrants.

Dear brothers and sisters, in light of these processes currently underway, the coming months offer a unique opportunity to advocate and support the concrete actions which I have described with four verbs. I invite you, therefore, to use every occasion to share this message with all political and social actors involved (or who seek to be involved) in the process which will lead to the approval of the two Global Compacts.

Today, August 15, we celebrate the Feast of the Assumption of Mary. The Holy Mother of God herself experienced the hardship of exile (Mt 2:13-15), lovingly accompanied her Son's journey to Calvary, and now shares eternally his glory. To her maternal intercession we entrust the hopes of all the world's migrants and refugees and the aspirations of the communities which welcome them, so that, responding to the Lord's supreme commandment, we may all learn to love the other, the stranger, as ourselves.

Vatican City, August 15, 2017
Solemnity of the Assumption of the B.V. Mary

Notes

1 Cf. Pius XII, Apostolic Constitution *Exsul Familia, Titulus Primus*, I.

2 Address to Participants in the International Forum on "Migration and Peace," February 21, 2017.

3 Cf. *Statement of the Permanent Observer of the Holy See to the 103rd Session of the Council of the IOM*, November 26, 2013.

4 Address to Participants in the International Forum on "Migration and Peace," February 21, 2017.

5 Cf. Benedict XVI, Encyclical Letter *Caritas in Veritate*, 47.

6 Cf. *Statement of the Permanent Observer of the Holy See to the 20th Session of the UN Human Rights Council*, June 22, 2012.

7 Cf. Benedict XVI, Encyclical Letter *Caritas in Veritate*, 62.

8 Cf. Pontifical Council for the Pastoral Care of Migrants and Itinerant People, Instruction *Erga Migrantes Caritas Christi*, 6.

9 Cf. Benedict XVI, Address to the Participants in the 6th World Congress for the Pastoral Care of Migrants and Itinerant People, November 9, 2009.

10 Cf. Benedict XVI, Message for the World Day of Migrants and Refugees (2010) and *Statement of the Permanent Observer of the Holy See to the 26th Ordinary Session of the Human Rights Council on the Human Rights of Migrants*, June 13, 2014.

11 Pontifical Council for the Pastoral Care of Migrants and Itinerant People and Pontifical Council *Cor Unum*, Welcoming Christ in Refugees and Forcibly Displaced Persons, 2013, 70.

12 Cf. Paul VI, Encyclical Letter *Populorum Progressio*, 14.

13 John Paul II, Encyclical Letter *Centesimus Annus*, 27.

14 Benedict XVI, Message for the World Day of Migrants and Refugees (2007).

15 Cf. Pontifical Council for the Pastoral Care of Migrants and Itinerant People and Pontifical Council *Cor Unum*, Welcoming Christ in Refugees and Forcibly Displaced Persons, 2013, 30-31.

16 John Paul II, *Message for the World Day of Migrants and Refugees* (2005).

Homily at Eucharistic Concelebration, World Day of Migrants and Refugees

Vatican Basilica

January 14, 2018

This year I wanted to celebrate the World Day of Migrants and Refugees with a Mass that invites and welcomes you especially who are migrants, refugees and asylum seekers. Some of you have recently arrived in Italy, others are long-time residents and work here, and still others make up the so-called "second-generation."

For everyone in this assembly, the Word of God has resonated and today invites us to deepen the special call that the Lord addresses to each one of us. As he did with Samuel (cf. 1 Sm 3:3b-10,19), he calls us by name—each one of us—and asks us to honor the fact that each of us has been created a unique and unrepeatable being, each different from the others and each with a singular role in the history of the world. In the Gospel (cf. Jn 1:35-42), the two disciples of John ask Jesus, "Where do you live?" (v. 38), implying that the reply to this question would determine their judgment upon the master from Nazareth. The response of Jesus is clear: *"Come and see!"* (v. 39), and opens up to a personal encounter which requires sufficient time to *welcome, to know* and *to acknowledge* the other.

In the Message for this year's World Day of Migrants and Refugees I have written, "Every stranger who knocks at our door is an opportunity for an encounter with Jesus Christ, who identifies with the welcomed and rejected strangers of every age (Mt 25:35, 43)." And for the stranger, the migrant, the refugee, the asylum seeker and the displaced person, every door in a new land is also an opportunity to encounter Jesus. His invitation "Come and see!" is addressed today to all of us, to local communities and to new arrivals. It is an invitation to overcome our fears so as to encounter the other, to welcome, to know and to acknowledge him or her. It is an invitation which offers the opportunity to draw near to the other and see where and how he or she lives. In today's world, for new arrivals to welcome, to know and to acknowledge means to know and respect the laws, the culture and the traditions of the countries that take them in. It even includes understanding their fears and apprehensions for the future. And for local communities to welcome, to know and to acknowledge newcomers means to open themselves without prejudices to their rich diversity, to understand the hopes and potential of the newly arrived as well as their fears and vulnerabilities.

True encounter with the other does not end with welcome, but involves us all in the three further actions which I spelled out in the Message for this Day: *to protect, to promote* and *to integrate*. In the true encounter with the neighbor, are we capable of recognizing Jesus Christ who is asking to be welcomed, protected, promoted and integrated? As the Gospel parable of the final judgment teaches us: the Lord was hungry, thirsty, naked, sick, a stranger and in prison—by some he was helped and by others not (cf. Mt 25:31-46). This true encounter with Christ is source of salvation, a salvation which should be announced and brought to all, as the apostle Andrew shows us. After revealing to his brother Simon, "We have found the Messiah" (Jn 1:41), Andrew brings him to Jesus so that Simon can have the same experience of encounter.

It is not easy to enter into another culture, to put oneself in the shoes of people so different from us, to understand their thoughts and their experiences. As a result we often refuse to encounter the other and raise barriers to defend ourselves. Local communities are sometimes afraid that the newly arrived will disturb the established order, will 'steal' something they have long labored to build up. And the newly arrived also have fears: they are afraid of confrontation, judgment, discrimination, failure. These fears are legitimate, based on doubts that are fully comprehensible from a human point of view. Having doubts and fears is not a sin. The sin is to allow these fears to determine our responses, to limit our choices, to compromise respect and generosity, to feed hostility and rejection. The sin is to refuse to encounter the other, the different, the neighbor, when this is in fact a privileged opportunity to encounter the Lord.

From this encounter with Jesus present in the poor, the rejected, the refugee, the asylum seeker, flows our prayer of today. It is a reciprocal prayer: migrants and refugees pray for local communities, and local communities pray for the newly arrived and for migrants who have been here longer. To the maternal intercession of Mary Most Holy we entrust the hopes of all the world's migrants and refugees and the aspirations of the communities which welcome them. In this way, responding to the supreme commandment of charity and love of neighbor, may we all learn to love the other, the stranger, as ourselves.

Homily at Holy Mass for Migrants

Altar of the Cathedra,
Saint Peter's Basilica

July 6, 2018

"You who trample upon the needy, and bring to ruin the poor of the land . . . Behold the days are coming . . . when I will send a famine on the land . . . a thirst for hearing the words of the Lord" (Amos 8:4, 11).

Today this warning of the prophet Amos is remarkably timely. How many of the poor are trampled on in our day! How many of the poor are being brought to ruin! All are the victims of that culture of waste that has been denounced time and time again. Among them, I cannot fail to include the migrants and refugees who continue to knock at the door of nations that enjoy greater prosperity.

Five years ago, during my visit to Lampedusa, recalling the victims lost at sea, I repeated that timeless appeal to human responsibility: "'Where is your brother? His blood cries out to me,' says the Lord. This is not a question directed to others; it is a question directed to me, to you, to each of us (Homily, July 8, 2013). Sadly, the response to this appeal, even if at times generous, has not been enough, and we continue to grieve thousands of deaths.

Today's Gospel acclamation contains Jesus' invitation: "Come to me, all who labor and are heavy laden, and I will give you rest" (Mt 11:28). The Lord promises refreshment and freedom to all the oppressed of our world, but he needs us to fulfil his promise. He needs our eyes to see the needs of our brothers and sisters. He needs our hands to offer them help. He needs our voice to protest the injustices committed thanks to the silence, often complicit, of so many. I should really speak of many silences: the silence of common sense; the silence that thinks, "it's always been done this way"; the silence of "us" as opposed to "you." Above all, the Lord needs our hearts to show his merciful love toward the least, the outcast, the abandoned, the marginalized.

In the Gospel we heard, Matthew tells us of the most important day in his life, the day Jesus called him. The Evangelist clearly records the Lord's rebuke to the Pharisees, so easily given to insidious murmuring: "Go and learn what this means, 'I desire mercy, and not sacrifice'" (9:13). It is a finger pointed at the sterile hypocrisy of those who do not want to "dirty the hands," like the priest or the Levite in the parable of the Good Samaritan. This is a temptation powerfully present in our own day. It takes the form of closing our hearts to those who have the right, just as we do, to security and dignified living conditions. It builds walls, real or virtual, rather than bridges.

Before the challenges of contemporary movements of migration, the only reasonable response is one of solidarity and mercy. A response less concerned with calculations, than with the need for an equitable distribution of responsibilities, an honest and sincere assessment of the alternatives and a prudent management. A just policy is one at the service of the person, of *every* person involved; a policy that provides for solutions that can ensure security, respect for the rights and dignity of all; a policy concerned for the good of one's own country, while taking into account that of others in an ever more interconnected world. It is to this world that the young look.

The Psalmist has shown us the right attitude to adopt in conscience before God: "I have chosen the way of faithfulness, I set your ordinances before me" (Ps 119:30). A commitment to faithfulness and right judgement that all of us hope to pursue together with government leaders in our world and all people of good will. For this reason, we are following closely the efforts of the international community to respond to the challenges posed by today's movements of migration by wisely combining solidarity and subsidiarity, and by identifying both resources and responsibilities. . . .

I wanted to celebrate the fifth anniversary of my visit to Lampedusa with you, who represent rescuers and those rescued on the Mediterranean Sea. I thank the rescuers for embodying in our day the parable of the

Good Samaritan, who stopped to save the life of the poor man beaten by bandits. He didn't ask where he was from, his reasons for travelling or his documents . . . he simply decided to care for him and save his life. To those rescued I reiterate my solidarity and encouragement, since I am well aware of the tragic circumstances that you are fleeing. I ask you to keep being witnesses of hope in a world increasingly concerned about the present, with little vision for the future and averse to sharing. With respect for the culture and laws of the country that receives you, may you work out together the path of integration.

I ask the Holy Spirit to enlighten our minds and to stir our hearts to overcome all fear and anxiety, and to make us docile instruments of the Father's merciful love, ready to offer our lives for our brothers and sisters, as the Lord Jesus did for each of us.